II

YET MORE GIBBERISH

Matthew Legare

The management takes no responsibility for mental or emotional
damage incurred by reading this book.
Thank you for your understanding.

copyright © 2021 by Matthew Legare

All rights reserved.

No part of this book may be reproduced or transmitted in any
form or by any means, electronic or mechanical, except for
the purpose of review and/or reference, without explicit
permission in writing from the publisher. Brief passages may
be excerpted for review and critical purposes.

Artisanal Gibberish logo design © 2021 by Matthew Legare

Cover design © 2021 by Niki Lenhart
nikilen-designs.com

Published by Unruly Voices
unrulyvoices.com

An imprint of Paper Angel Press
paperangelpress.com

ISBN 978-1-953469-54-0 (Trade Paperback)

FIRST EDITION

10 9 8 7 6 5 4 3 2 1

This tome is dedicated to all the people who put up with this nonsense, especially my parents Kathy and Roger (still bewildered), and my wife, Ami.

And to everyone out there whose heads work like this — see? If I can make a book, anybody can!

MYTH
&
FANTASY

Many Fractious Mightily
Flippant Montages Forming
Silly Poems

Dungeon

My friend was imprisoned by the King.
He got thrown in the dungeon.

He felt pretty resentful about it,
so he was in a dudgeon in the dungeon.

It affected his personality, making him distrustful.
It made him a curmudgeon in a dudgeon in the dungeon.

The guards were pretty mean to him, too.
Frequently, they used a bludgeon on the curmudgeon in a dudgeon in the dungeon.

They had to be careful, though, not to hit him too hard, lest they incur serious injury.
They didn't want to cause a concussion from the percussion of the bludgeon on the curmudgeon in a dudgeon in the dungeon.

That kind of treatment could give a dungeon a bad name.
It would be a blot on the escutcheon to get a concussion from the percussion of the bludgeon on the curmudgeon in a dudgeon in the dungeon.

Muse

A spirit of inspiration is called a muse.

If your spirit of inspiration confounds you, that would be a bemusing muse.

And if you felt hard done by because of it, that would be a bemusing muse abuse.

Listening to someone laboring under such a spirit might be bemusing muse abuse confusion …

And I'm hoping that all this stuff I'm writing will bring bemusing muse abuse confusion amusement.

BEORN

There is a character in J. R. R. Tolkein's book *The Hobbit*, a skin-changer named Beorn, spelled B E O R N and pronounced "BEE-orn".

If he had a bugle, it'd be the Beorn Horn.
He doesn't play it much, so it's a forlorn Beorn horn …
It's kinda plain, and he wants to make it fancier.
He wishes to adorn the forlorn Beorn horn.
Perhaps, he thinks, if he does this, then it's more likely that the adorned forlorn Beorn horn will be worn.

Stage Combat

Stage combat is the art of portraying violence on stage, so, you're presenting a stage fight.

In some shows, there's a lot of violence, and it's easy to lose track, so you have to make sure you're presenting the right fight.

You have to make sure you're throwing the correct punch at the correct time in the correct spot to ensure you're displaying the right fight smite.

If you don't, well that'll make the show look bad; it could suffer from a right fight smite blight.

This would result in your fleeing the stage, or a right fight smite blight flight.

You'd be fleeing the stage out of terror — the right fight smite blight flight fright.

CRITTERS

A Cacophonous Collection of
Contrived Compositions
Concerning Animals

Parrots

Pirates like to have birds with them on their voyages.
They're particularly fond of parrots.
If there's more than one bird on a ship, the birds should be of equal worth.

The pirates must strive for parrot parity.
The pirates have to be earnest in this effort, lest it lapse into parrot parity parody.

Usually this happens when one pirate mocks another, and then gets a friend to join him, so we have a pair of parrot parity parodies.

On a small enough ship, everyone winds up with a bird and the mocking winds up becoming almost circular — so everyone is mocking everyone else, which results in a pair of parrot parity parody paradox.

CARIBOU

If a Caribou has an SO, this would be the Caribou's Boo.

If the Caribou's SO had an injury, that'd be a Caribou's Boo's Boo-Boo.

If the injury were to the Caribou, and the Caribou identified as male, that'd be the Caribou's Boo's Beau's Boo-Boo.

Tying a ribbon on it would result in a Caribou's Boo's Beau's Boo-Boo Bow.

If the Caribou's SO sang Rubber Biscuit while the Caribou wore a ribbon on his injury, that'd be a Caribou's Boo's Beau's Boo-Boo Bow Bow-Bow-Bow …

AAAAND if the Caribou was named after a French Poet of the 1800s who is credited with translating the works of Edgar Allen Poe into French … that'd be a CariBaudlidaire's Boo's Beau's Boo-Boo Bow Bow-Bow-Bow …

AAAAND if the Caribou that was named after a French Poet of the 1800s who is credited with translating the works of Edgar Allen Poe into French was somewhere in the Atlantic Ocean in the tropics … it's be the Caribbean CariBaudlidaire's Boo's Beau's Boo-Boo Bow Bow-Bow-Bow …

CATTLE

A very old word for 'cattle' is 'kine'.
If your cattle are nice to you, then they're kind kine.
I would think that most dairy farmers would prefer the kind kind of kine.
But, if that sort was in short supply, then reasonably nice cows would do ... the kind of kind kind of kine.
In Hawaii, especially if you weren't sure of the right word to use to describe them, they'd be da kine kind of kind kind of kine.
Which, I suppose, means that if there was a German dairy farmer in Hawaii and his uncertainly sort-of-nice cattle had calves, those would be da kine kind kind of kind of kine ... kinder.

VACATION

I really need to get out some.
I need a vacation.
I think I'd like to go crabbing.

That would make it a crustacean vacation.

There's probably at least one place out on the coast where I could do that.

A crustacean vacation station.

The person who runs it probably does it as their job, full-time.
It's that person's crustacean vacation station vocation.

As with any business line, there's probably a group that advocates for them.

A crustacean vacation station vocation organization.

But, with the changing climate, I'm not sure how long such groups will continue to exist,
due to crustacean vacation station vocation organization ablation.

This probably bugs the people who do this for a living,
resulting in crustacean vacation station vocation organization ablation frustration.

And considering what a novel job this is, people give them grief about their annoyance … crustacean vacation station vocation organization ablation frustration degradation.

PEOPLE

Properly Prepared Peripatetic
Ponderings of Folks
I Might Know

BEGGAR

I know a professional beggar in the village of Scarborough.
Well, to be accurate, she's a professional groveller.
She'll grovel on any surface, including a surface made of small rough stones.
She will in fact grovel in the gravel.

She's made enough from grovelling in the gravel to afford to build a small home.
She has a hovel from the grovel in the gravel.

While it's not big enough to keep a large pet, she has domesticated a small bug.
She has a weevil in the hovel from the grovel in the gravel.

Sadly, there are laws against that sort of thing. Which means that some poor constable had to be assigned the retrieval of the weevil from the hovel from the grovel in the gravel.

This caused some discontent among the other licensed beggars.
Resulting in an upheaval from the retrieval of the weevil from the hovel from the grovel in the gravel.

Due to all the hubbub, that particular statute has been rescinded.
There was a reprieval due to the upheaval from the retrieval of the weevil in the hovel from the grovel in the gravel.

Fakir

In the far east, a religious ascetic who lives solely on alms is known as a fakir.

If you were pretending to be one, you'd be a faker fakir.

If you really *were* a religious ascetic who was *pretending* to be one, you'd be a fake faker fakir.

If enough people contributed to you via alms that you could afford multiple vehicles, you might be a four car fake faker fakir.

If all of those automobiles got T-boned, then you'd be a forked four car fake faker fakir.

And if you got really popular on the Internet because someone posted an article about you on an aggregation site, you'd be a farked forked four car fake faker fakir.

LANDSKNECHT

German mercenaries of the 1300s to 1600s were called *Landsknechts*.

When they networked with each other to find work, that was when the Landsknecht connected.

If they did not work through an intermediary, that was a Landsknecht direct connect.

If a bunch of them got together to network, that was a Landsknecht direct connect collect.

Sometimes, a German mercenary wasn't well liked by the others; this resulted in a Landsknecht direct connect collect reject.

This refusal to network would make the rejected mercenary very sad, resulting in a Landsknecht direct connect collect reject verklempt.

Contagious

Apparently my gibberish causes other people to compose stuff like this, or at least add to the things I've, uh, "written" …

Apparently it's contagious.
Or at least, reading or hearing my gibberish makes people brave enough to add to it,

So it's a courageous contagious.
And since this phenomenon is pretty "out there" …
That'd make it an outrageous courageous contagious.
And there's no telling how long this outrageous courageous contagious will plague us.

Pole

My friend is of Polish heritage.

He'd like to erect an obelisk in honor of his heritage, but due to budget considerations, he's had to settle for erecting a pole.

It is a pole pole.

He is not entirely settled on what kind of pole he wants to put up, so he's asking his friends and neighbors to choose their preference from a list.

This is a Pole pole poll.

The booth in which he has asked his friends and neighbors to choose in is lit electrically.
The power source is a battery, or a Pole pole poll *pile.*[*]

Each end of the battery is a Pole pole poll pile pole.

Unfortunately, due to a short in the wiring, dark smoke has obscured the voting area.
This is a Pole pole poll pile pole pall.

---

[*] The original term for a battery was *pile*, in French, because a battery is literally a stack of alternating metals and, if you said it in French, it sounded intellectual.

Pendant

Sometimes I think that pedants should have some kind of signifying emblem or something, worn around a chain; a pedant pendant.

If it were fancy, it'd be a resplendent pedant pendant.
If it were fancy, and the pedant only travelled by walking, it could be a resplendent peripatetic pedant pendant.

If, for some reason, they chose a legume as the emblem noted on the device, it'd be a resplendent peripatetic peanut pedant pendant.

And if this someone got to be *such* a stickler that you didn't need to see them wearing such an emblem to know the kind of person they were, they'd have become resplendent peripatetic peanut pedant pendant transcendent.

Vision

My company has recently worked to develop a short
   phrase to describe what the company will do in the
   future. They have created a Vision Statement.

However, there is already some discussion about
   changing it.
Some people want some revision of the vision.

This has caused some conflict.
There has been division in the revision of the vision.

This has caused a certain amount of excitement.
There has been frisson about the division in the
   revision of the vision.

Because the company has a tendency toward caution,
   some folks want to cut out the causes for excitement
   — an incision of the frisson about the division in the
   revision of the vision.

But to do that, they'd need this removal to be
   performed by a third party.
They'd have to commission an incision of the frisson
   about the division in the revision of the vision.

FOOD

A Felicitously Flung Family of Flibbertigibbet Food Nonsense

Knish

My friend likes these little bread rolls with fillings.

I think it's called a *knish*.

He'll have them as a snack.

So that's a knish nosh.

Sometimes he puts a little chocolate glaze on it.

That's a knish nosh ganache.

He's pretty good with making designs, so he drew the Hindu God of Openings on the roll with the glaze.

That's a Ganesh knish nosh ganache.

He likes to eat them while playing retro kids games, like one from the 70's where you knock colored ping pong balls through hoops into the other player's side.

That'd make the roll decoration a gnip-gnop Ganesh knish nosh ganache.

And if he also has a sausage made from dried meats while playing this game and eating this bread roll …

It'd be a kishka gnip-gnop Ganesh knish nosh ganache.

Apparently they're pretty tasty.

So that's a delish kishka gnip-gnop Ganesh knish nosh ganache … b'gosh!

Microwave

I had to microwave my lunch today; there was a reheatin' for the eatin'.

But it wasn't sufficiently warmed up to eat, so I had to reheat it again; there was a repeatin' of the reheatin' for the eatin'.

This isn't the first instance of this happening, and I'm worried that the microwave may need to be replaced.

I can't make the decision on my own, so our company had a meetin' about the repeatin' of the reheatin' for the eatin'.

Frankly, if the nuker can be fixed, I'd be fine with that, I just want to cut back on the times I have to run it.

My goal, post-meetin', is a depletin' of the repeatin' of the reheatin' for the eatin'.

LUMBERJACK BEER

They're making a beer specifically for woodsmen now; it's a logger lager.

The brewery documents all the sales of this beverage; they do so in their logger lager log.

Sometimes it takes a while to tally up the sales

Which results in a laggy logger lager log.

But once it's caught up, I'm sure that'll make the laggy logger lager log longer.

Considering how much effort went into keeping the document, it's likely to be a lovingly lauded longer laggy logger lager log.

After reading this aloud, I need a lovingly lauded longer laggy logger logger log lozenge.

(Thanks to Claire for the last two lines.)

Sous-Vide

If you prep food for cooking, you're a sous chef.

If you prep food for cooking and that food is going to be cooked in a sealed bag in temperature-controlled water for a long period of time, that would make you a sous-vide sous chef.

If you were a member of a particular Native American tribe who prepared food for cooking which would be cooked in a sealed bag in temperature-controlled water for a long period of time, that would make you a Sioux sous-vide sous chef.

If you studied this technique long enough, you might get a Ph.D. and become Doctor Sous[*] the Sioux Sous-Vide Sous Chef.

And if the meal you were preparing was for Phil Collins of Genesis, that might make you Doctor Sous, the Sioux sous-vide Sususdio sous chef.

(inspired by Snipe)

---

[*] Yes, I know, it's a pun, or play on words. If you've gotten this far into the book, I honestly don't think you have any grounds to be upset by it.

Chickens

If you work on a farm and your job is to take care of the chickens, you are a chicken tender.

And if you have someone do the housework while you're caring for the chickens, that person would be a chicken tender tender.

If that person felt fondness for you, that person would be a tender chicken tender tender.

And you would pay that person in tender chicken tender tender legal tender.

That money would be carried across water in a tender chicken tender tender legal tender tender.

And the contract to carry that money on a boat across the water to pay the kind person who takes care of you while you take care of the chickens would be a tender chicken tender tender legal tender tender tender tender.

How did you find the kind person to take care of you while you take care of the chickens?

Tender chicken tender tender legal tender tender tender tender tinder.

CACTUS

A cactus growing in the Himalayas is a Nepali Nopales.
Most people aren't fond of them.
They'd be all "Nope!" on the Nepali Nopales.
Although some folks might feel otherwise. Especially the rich.
Rather than be all nope on the Nepali Nopales, Noble Nabobs in Napa might Nosh Nightly on Nepali Nopales.

Stollen

In Germany, they make a bread containing nuts, spices, and candied fruit. This bread is called "Stollen".

It's in very high demand, and some bakers pack their bread so densely with the fillings that it becomes larger than average.

This would be a swollen Stollen.

A bread of this magnitude can cause other bakers to become envious and want to snatch it away, resulting in a Swollen Stolen Stollen.

If the bread thief is pursued by the constabulary, they may be motivated to ditch the evidence by chucking it over a fence, resulting in a Thrown Swollen Stolen Stollen.

This happens so often that the constabulary has instituted a small group of officers to go looking for formerly-snatched hurled bread products ... and they go Thrown Swollen Stolen Stollen Patrollin'.

They do this in vehicles which use internal combustion, powered by Thrown Swollen Stolen Stollen Patrollin' Petroleum.

STEIN

I have a lidded drinking vessel from Germany.

It is a stein.

It has a portrait of the author of *An Autobiography of Alice B Toklas* on it.

It's a Gertrude Stein stein.

It's in collectible condition.

It's a fine Gertrude Stein stein.

I don't use it for beer, really. I'm not a big beer drinker.

It's a fine Gertrude Stein wine stein.

It was made as a promotional item by a designer of *haute couture*.

It's a Calvin Klein fine Gertrude Stein wine stein.

And I own it.

Yep, the Calvin Klein fine Gertrude Stein wine stein is mine.

REALLY JUST NOUNS

... what it says on the label.
My editor got this far
and gave up.

TCHOTCHKE

My friend collects little decorative doodads, or tchotchkes.

He has one that's in the shape of a key for a cathedral. It's a church key tchotchke.

It also doubles as a bottle opener, so in bar terms it's a "Church Key" church key tchotchke.

He had to hunt it down online, and use a "Church Key" church key tchotchke search tree.

The hunt got so desperate that he wound up paying for a service to find it, requiring a "Church Key" church key tchotchke search tree search fee.

DAGGER

Dying on stage is not easy.

Particularly if you get stabbed by a big knife, or dagger.

It's not enough to just flop down where you're stabbed. No, you have to move around a bit to increase the drama.

Hence, the dagger stagger.

Those actors who can pull off a particularly poignant trip around the stage after being shanked can be said to have dagger stagger swagger.

However, the stage manager will frequently have to signal to the actor that yes, that's enough and he can fall down now.

Making the stage manager a dagger stagger swagger flagger.

Occasionally, an actor just goes too far, and might have to have a sack pulled down over him so he can be hauled off stage by a minion of the stage manager, or a dagger stagger swagger flagger bagger.

Tome

I've been writing poetry for a while now.

In a nod to tradition, once I've composed them, I keep my works in a blank book.

It's my poem tome.

While I do a lot of travelling and I write wherever I am, I tend to leave that book where I live.

It's my home poem tome.

To be honest, sometimes I take the book with me, but I always bring it back to my house.

So it's my roaming home poem tome.

I've sometimes thought about making a copy, or cloning my roaming home poem tome.

If I do, I'll have to put my address in the new copy, so people will know where the clone of my roaming home poem tome is from.

AirBNBBRB

I want to open a service to rent places where people can go to be idle while online.

I want to call it AirBNBBRB.

If they had a roast beef place in there, it'd be an AirBNBBRBArby's.

If it was established in a nudist colony, it'd be a BareAirBNBBRBArby's.

Probably not a lot of them around, so it'd be a RareBareAirBNBBRBArby's.

And if it was licensed by a toy line that featured ursines with emblems on their chest,

that'd be a CareBearRareBareAirBNBBRBArby's.

CARBINE

My friend has a firearm. It's a carbine.
It's made from spun fiber. It's a carbon carbine.
It's a duplicate of one that was made earlier.
It's a carbon copy carbon carbine.
It was given to him by someone who irritated a Spanish speaker.
It's a cabrón carbon copy carbon carbine.

Yeet

There's this odd bit of slang going around that means to
    throw or hurl something.
The word, I think, is *yeet*.

This got me to thinking.

If something was thrown by the Road-Runner's
    nemesis in the cartoons,
That would be a 'yote yeet.
Said 'yote would be, as it were, yeeting.
And if said nemesis was on a boat,
Then that would be the 'yote yeeting from a yacht.
If said nemesis hurled some fermented milk product
    from the boat,
That would be the 'yote yeeting the yacht's yogurt
Possibly eliciting the following expression of surprise
    from an old-fashioned passer-by
"Yoinks! The 'yote's yeeting the yacht's yogurt!"

Earrings

Someone has made earrings that are little sculptures of ears.

They are ear earrings.

If someone pierced the lobes of those earrings, you could wear ear earring rings.

If someone wrote a song about those, and someone else made that the sound their phone made when they got a call, that would be the ear earring ring ringtone.

Board

Sometimes I write this stuff by hand, and other times, I use a keyboard.

I tend to swap out devices that I use for writing, so I do not get keyboard bored.

If I succumbed to ennui from using the same device all the time, I'd be keyboard bored floored.

If my ennui-driven pratfall from being so overwhelmed with ennui from using the same device over and over was really impressive, I might win a keyboard bored floored award.

I'd tether it to the mantle using a keyboard bored floored award cord.

I have a rapier over my mantle already, so I'd use it to defend this plaque.

The rapier would become my keyboard bored floored award cord sword.

Tassle

Burlesque dancers deal with a lot of things that most folks don't have to contend with on a regular basis.
Like tassels.
These things are kind of problematic - sometimes they don't swing the way you want them to, sometimes they spin the wrong way.
Burlesque dancers have tassel hassles.
If someone's in the business for long enough, they'll encounter just about every way one of these things can go wrong.
They'd amass a passel of tassel hassles.
It turns out there's a Burlesque Museum in a little city in Central Germany where these things are documented.
It's in an old, fortified building.
Yes, there is a Castle in Cassel where they've amassed a passel of tassel hassles.
It only has one servant though.
He's the Vassal of the Castle in Cassel where they've amassed a passel of tassel hassles.

About the Author

Matthew Legare (aka "Tobias the Adequate") is what happens when you tell someone they can be anything they want to be — but provide no further guidance. A performer and creator of "stuff" since he was able to stand upright, he can check off the boxes for "actor", "writer", "director", "renter of fishing boats", "painter of bathrooms", "wrangler of technology", and a number of other jobs which look good in an author's biography.

Unable to stop making stuff up (he's tried; we checked), Matthew is credited (or blamed) with a number of radio plays and spoken-word performances at fairs, festivals, and themed gatherings. Since so many people responded to "I'm a magician." with "Oh? What instrument do you play?", Mr. Legare has branched into geeky, nerdy, goofy music with his "Troubadork" show, streaming regularly and coming to the aforementioned gatherings.

Matthew lives in an undisclosed location in San Antonio, Texas, with his extremely patient and supportive partner, Ami, and somewhere between zero and too many cats.

Other Gibberish

by Matthew Legare

Man vs. Poetry. Poetry may be ahead on points.

www.ingramcontent.com/pod-product-compliance
Lightning Source LLC
Chambersburg PA
CBHW021452070526
44577CB00002B/374